There's no other city in America quite like New York. For sure,
LA packs plenty of glitz and glamour, and San Fran has been
stealing hearts since the early 1960s, but there's something about
the chaotic, fast-paced, anything goes melting-pot that is NYC
that never ceases to enthrall me. From that aspiring singer on
a train, or a 4am pastrami bagel, to the more than eight million
innovative residents, there's something bewitching in the air.

It's a city that challenges you to search out and listen to the
many multi-ethnic and multi-generational stories that are told
with great pride (justifiably so, because they worked hard for
it, dammit). From family-owned businesses to studios of a...
funded by Kickstarter, there ar...
may develop a serious case o...
worry not, for few come to Ne...
your get-around guide o...

the hunt new york city writer

joanna kang

JoAnna Kang admits she had to pluck up courage to make the cross-country
move from Portland to New York. She finally confronted NYC's cramped living
and long workdays in exchange for relishing a 24-hour glutton's paradise, where
diverse creativity is awakened. She has written for *Portland Monthly Magazine*
and *Edible Manhattan*, and when not hard at work, she enjoys recreating delicious
recipes from Elizabeth David cookbooks, fogging up a glass case of smoked fish
and caviar in her local deli, or browsing the shops and art shows on her doorstep
in the Lower East Side.

where to lay your weary head

Rest up, relax and recharge

DISTRIKT HOTEL
Utilitarian in Midtown West

342 West 40th Street (between 8th and 9th) / +1 212 706 6100 / distrikthotel.com

Double from $395

Distrikt Hotel is for the savvy traveler whose itinerary is typed out to the minute, hoping to catch every attraction in town. Located between Port Authority and Times Square, every major train line is in close proximity so guests can commute with ease. With New York City-themed décor, including a 12-foot living wall in the lobby representing Central Park, and high-class hospitality and facilities, Distrikt Hotel will rest weary heads and tired tourist feet in style.

LAFAYETTE HOUSE
Pre-war Nolita brownstone

38 East 4th Street (between Lafayette and Cooper) / +1 212 505 8100
lafayettenyc.com

Double from $245

Formerly a pre-war apartment complex, the Lafayette House has 15 cozy bedrooms. Each one has a functioning marble fireplace, and some even have a kitchenette and private patio, so if you'd like to pretend you're in your very own NY pad, snag one of those. I overhear a lot of tourists say, "I love visiting NYC, but I'd never want to live here." Well, after a night availing of Lafayette's charms, guests just might find themselves curiously scrolling through real estate listings over their morning coffee.

THE INN AT IRVING PLACE
Historic-home hospitality

56 Irving Place (between 17th and 18th) / +1 212 533 4600 / innatirving.com

Double from $445

Built in 1834, this terraced-house hotel is a refuge from the city. Minus possessing the coveted key for the private, fenced Gramercy Park located merely a block away, guests will feel right at home in this clandestine, sans-sign, Victorian style townhouse. A refined interior including 12 guest rooms and the elegant Lady Mendl's Tea Salon, this is a perfect place for a quiet getaway. Pinkies up.

THE KING & GROVE WILLIAMSBURG

Contemporary luxury in an urban retreat

160 North 12th Street (between Berry and Bedford) / +1 718 218 7500
kingandgrove.com

Double from $205

Water-babies will find it difficult to resist the three-season, salt-water outdoor swimming pool here, one of the largest in NYC. As at the sister hotel in the heart of the city, The King & Grove Williamsburg offers luxurious hospitality and stylish furnishings in the form of bamboo floors, neutral beige and gray accents, and marble bathrooms.

THE NOMAD HOTEL

THE MARLTON
West Village beatnik abode

5 West 8th Street (between 5th and 6th) / +1 212 321 0100 / marltonhotel.com

Double from $295

How apropos for a neighborhood known for its excruciatingly adorable cafés to now have a charming Parisian-ascribed boutique hotel – that also happens to serve raw almond cappuccinos at its espresso bar. Well, I don't know how Parisian that last part sounded, but The Marlton does deserve full credits for its romantic décor of marble floors, charming molding and literary history. Over a century old, it has housed the likes of John Barrymore, Jack Kerouac and Lenny Bruce. Rooms are small, but comfortably stylish – ideal for artists on a budget.

THE NOMAD HOTEL
Chic comfort with a top-notch restaurant

1170 Broadway (between 27th and 28th) / +1 212 796 1500 / thenomadhotel.com

Double from $395

Who can resist The NoMad's cocktail bar or the chance to snuggle with a book in their library? Or enjoying the luxurious roast chicken stuffed with foie gras in their constantly buzzing and overbooked NoMad restaurant? Or dropping by for its weekly live jazz performance of rousing 1920s tunes held on the second floor? Lucky guests, because they can do all this knowing that once all the fun's been had, bed is but an elevator-ride away. The rooms have a classic, timeless style inspired by the Parisian-apartment home of the designer's youth.

WYTHE HOTEL
Boutique chic in Williamsburg

80 Wythe Avenue (corner of North 11th) / + 1 718 782 2945 / wythehotel.com

Double from $275

The Ides, the Wythe Hotel's rooftop bar, arguably has one of the best skyline views of Manhattan, where the jagged rows of colossal, concrete stalagmites rise from the single narrow peninsula. The hotel's designer wallpaper (from Flavor Paper) casually cushions the gritty, industrial use of exposed brick and planks of dark wood, and the beds are made of pine reclaimed from the building – a blend of chic grunge brought to you by a collaboration of the best local artists, designers and architects.

east village and lower east side

financial district, tribeca

As of late, a barrage of strollers and young professionals enjoys TriBeCa's quaint, cobblestone streets, beautiful waterfront views and industrial sun-lit lofts. Straight-shave barbers and shoe shiners still remain open for Wall Street worker bees in the Financial District; while in East Village and Lower East Side (L.E.S.) – once home to vagabonds, drug dealers and defunct fabric stores – NYU dormitories and burgeoning independent art galleries abound. Here was the birthplace of artistic movements, punk rock and protests, and it remains a center of counterculture despite gentrification.

1   Chambers Street Wines (off map)
2   Cocoron
3   Fabulous Fanny's
4   Hengst
5   Korin (off map)
6   Maiden Lane
7   Maryam Nassir Zadeh
8   Mondo Cane (off map)
9   Pilgrim
10 Russ & Daughters
11 Spiritual America (off map)
12 Still House
13 Top Hat
14 Top Hops

CHAMBERS STREET WINES

Unparalleled biodynamic and organic wine selection

148 Chambers Street (between Broadway and Greenwich)
+1 212 227 1434 / chambersstwines.com / Open daily

Oftentimes, stepping into a wine store can be as daunting as attempting to adapt to a foreign country, learning the language and understanding the culture. I've certainly encountered a few vino experts who rattle off Robert Parker quotes, their faces turning the color of grapes when I can't recall the number of hectares in Château-Chalon. Happily at Chambers Street Wines, such snobbery does not exist. The staff is passionate in educating and challenging drinkers to step out of their personal DOC (Denominazione Origin of Comfort). Head over to the 15-foot-long shelf of niche Champagne labels and start your journey of discovery.

COCORON

Where soba takes center stage

61 Delancey Street (between Allen and Eldridge) / **+1 212 925 5220**
cocoron-soba.com / **Closed Monday**

Cocoron, a tiny 14-seater with four bandana-wearing line cooks huddled around a single gas stove, can put tummy grumbling on speakerphone. The anticipation is like watching soba Olympics. There's the broth taster, noodle expert, meat guy and garnish guru. With all this methodology, the likelihood of an inconsistent bowl is, well, highly unlikely. Though appropriately sized for its location on the edge of L.E.S. – a.k.a. Little Elbow Space – the sweet salinity of bonito broth and silky strands of buckwheat noodles will surely touch people's hearts, because the name Cocoron means just that: heartwarming.

FABULOUS FANNY'S

Eccentric wonderland for the visually impaired

335 East 9th Street (between 1st and 2nd) / **+1 212 533 0637**
store.fabulousfannys.com / **Open daily**

In second grade I became a secret squinter. Though sitting right in front of the chalkboard inadvertently typecast me as an overachiever, it wasn't until my mother caught on that I was forced to wear thick, red-rimmed, bifocal glasses that created years of provocation. Stepping into Fabulous Fanny's was like post-traumatic glasses-wearing therapy. The staff offers honest opinions to help you choose the right frames, the stock of which ranges from vintage 18th-century to modern designs. The selection is so massive, you'll wish you really had four-eyes to go through it all. Time to trade in my bifocals for vintage Emmanuelle Khanh and forever rid myself of torturous elementary school memories.

HENGST

New York designed and crafted womenswear

70 East 1st Street (between 1st and 2nd) / +1 212 375 1549
hengstnyc.com / Closed Monday

Marilyn's white dress; Audrey's black sheath; Katharine's tweed pants. Clothing may not maketh the woman, but it sure can tell one hell of a story. With wisps of silk, architectural shapes and stunning construction, the pieces in Hengst's little East Village shop hum with narrative potential. Slip on an aqua crêpe de chine dress and you're sweeping into the opening of your new gallery. Throw on the black silk smoking jacket and you're holding court at a literary salon, martini in hand. Give me a shout if you ever find yourself at the Met on a Sunday afternoon; I'll be the one admiring the modernist work in cropped satin flat-front trousers.

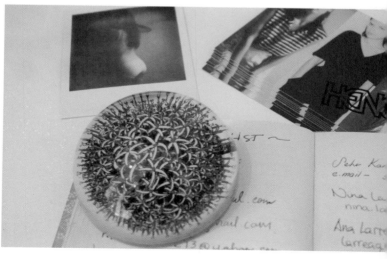

KORIN

Japanese forged knives

57 Warren Street (between West Broadway and Church Street)
+1 212 587 7021 / korin.com / Open daily

My craving for anything grilled increases exponentially with
awareness that barbecuing on an NY tenement rooftop is subject
to eviction. Growing up, my father, the grill master, lectured me on
the grades of charcoal and the importance of a sharp butchering
knife. Korin happens to offer both, including three different types
of Japanese charcoal and a collection of Japan-forged knives that
follows the Sakai knife craftsmanship – famous for its samurai swords.
Custom sharpening is offered by Master Chiharu Sugai via a whetting
wheel; one of two in the world that he himself designed.

MAIDEN LANE

Cured and specialty canned seafood

162 Avenue B (corner of East 10th) / +1 646 755 8911
themaidenlane.com / Open daily

The Whitefish Salad at Maiden Lane blows tuna between slices of bread
outta the water. Well, obviously. It might also have to do with the
co-owners, Naills Fallon and Gareth Maccubbin, curing their own fish,
as well as sourcing some from ACME Smoked Fish. Who knew imported
sardines and cockles, both from beautifully labeled cans, could taste so
grand. Oil-slicked fillets from Jose Gourmet in Portugal, sold exclusively
in the U.S. at Maiden Lane, gracefully swim amongst crunchy crudités.
Surrender to the nautical theme and savor the pinewood planks of
delicate sliced lox, creamy whitefish and uninterrupted glasses of briny
sherry. Chin-chin!

MARYAM NASSIR ZADEH

Contemporary women's clothing

123 Norfolk Street (corner of Rivington) / **+1 212 673 6405**
mnzstore.com / **Open daily**

In this beautiful store, the rows of gossamer silks and hand-tailored
wool suits are carefully arranged, as if the hangers were painstakingly
hung at a futuristic exhibition in the textile wing of a museum. Designer
and store co-owner Maryam Nassir Zadeh's relationship with art and
travel is what makes this boutique a true shopping destination. Stepping
into what feels more like a stark, white art gallery allows shoppers
to stop and admire an accessory, a blanket or a shift dress, as if it's a
colorful Kandinsky painting.

MONDO CANE

A world of design, antique and modern

174 Duane Street (corner of Greenwich) / **+1 212 219 9244**
mondocane.com / **Closed Sunday**

Working with reputable designers and architects and specializing in décor that spans over a century makes Mondo Cane something of an authority within the design world. Handsome objects of art, furniture, lighting and homeware are displayed in a cohesive manner within its spacious TriBeCa store; and, like an enticing installation should, the layout keeps the eye moving. The good news is nearly everything on site is for sale, so you can take all your favorites home. And if you simply can't wait until you are next in NYC, Mondo Cane also showcases throughout the country, including participating in Palm Springs' annual Modernism Week.

PILGRIM

The ultimate in vintage

70 Orchard Street (between Grand and Broome) / **+1 212 463 7720**
pilgrimnyc.com / **Open daily**

When expanding one's collection of prized possessions, whether it's an obscure LP or mint-condition Hermès scarf, there's always someone who has the know-how in acquiring desired recherché. Luckily co-owners of Pilgrim, Richard Ives and Brian Bennett, are seasoned sleuths in procuring vintage Chanel and creating ready-to-wear lines under Ives' own label. There are no noses yanked up by the strings of sales commissions here. No, there's only clever fashion advice and storytelling of style lore that'll steer loyal patrons clear of any buyer's remorse. It's only a matter of time before Ives' own beloved, feminine designs will also become collectibles.

RUSS & DAUGHTERS

Golden child of appetizing shops

179 East Houston Street (between Orchard and Allen)
+1 212 475 4880 / russanddaughters.com / Open daily

Founder Joel Russ originally began his entrepreneurial venture behind a pushcart, from which witty, friendly service and fish expertise became, 100 years later, a store that The Smithsonian Institute tributes as "a part of New York's cultural heritage". Russ & Daughters maintains family traditions and is a historical and culinary golden child among NYC's mouthwatering Jewish shops. There's a reason why the best always outlasts the rest. To watch the venerable staff hand-slice velvety, paper-thin, smoked salmon while sampling hand-whipped scallion cream cheese is worth every minute of waiting in a congested, all-day queue. The knife skills, the banter, a handful of Hopjes, and of course the fish are all impossible to resist. I gush, but there is simply no other place as magical as Russ & Daughters, if you ask me.

SPIRITUAL AMERICA

Home of independent labels

5 Rivington Street (between Bowery and Chrystie) / **+1 212 960 8564**
spiritualamericanyc.com / **Open daily**

Claire Lemétais, the owner of Spiritual America, is one ace of a buyer. She's astute at reeling in hard-to-find indie labels from small, exclusive showrooms such as Hussein Chalayan. Some nurse-themed 1970's novels, of the type that inspired the artist Richard Prince, curiously accent the boutique's minimalist white walls, as trapezoidal succulents provide an elemental and geometric accessory within the showroom. After a visit to Spiritual America, it'd be no surprise if Claire inspires you to open up your own shop someday – or to simply buy everything in sight. I'll vote for the latter.

STILL HOUSE

Precious gifts for friends and home

117 East 7th Street (between Avenue A and 1st) / +1 212 539 0200
stillhousenyc.com / Open daily

Still House evokes everything the name describes: tranquility, warmth
and simplicity. Owner Urte Tylaite carefully curates stunning jewelry,
home goods and creative gifts. The former is spectacular, and always
affordably priced. Pieces range from thin gold rings delicately dotted with
precious, tiny diamonds to geometrically bold earrings. And even returning
customers who just try on the same thing during every visit (i.e., me), are
welcomed by the gracious Urte who acts as if she's hosting an intimate
reception, and who answers all questions eruditely and with a smile — a
dying trait in today's commercial world.

TOP HAT

A haven of home décor and stationery

245 Broome Street (between Ludlow and Orchard)   +1 212 677 4240
tophatnyc.com / Open daily

I popped into Top Hat to find a small gift for a fellow stationery lover.
Little did I know, owner Nina Allen offers more than the average pencil case.
It's a place where delicate French lace is sold by the yard. Oh, and colorful
Italian Ellepi staplers and the largest MT masking tape assortment I've ever
seen. If clerical workers walked the runway, Top Hat would be there to clad
them with all things necessary — and make them look good, too. From
intricate laser-cut bookmarks to Maison Martin Margiela notebooks, Top Hat
carries alluring, minimalist designs from all over the world.

TOP HOPS

Converter of beer snobs

94 Orchard Street (between Broome and Delancey) / **+1 212 254 4677**
tophops.com / **Open daily**

This is the most egalitarian craft bar I've ever stepped into. It's a place where hipsters, foodies and craft beer geeks saddle up along the bar to marvel at the 20 rotating taps from around the world. It's also a place to laugh at the flabbergasted blind tasters when Budweiser emerges a favorite among elitists. More importantly, there's an amazing beer list, with 700 bottles and cans for your tasting pleasure. And if all that imbibing whets your palate, delicious local snacks make for a perfect accompaniment. What's better than supporting local businesses and small breweries? I'll say cheers to that.

BA XUYÊN
4222 8th Avenue (corner of 43rd), +1 718 633 6601, no website
weekend brunch 7.30am – 6.30pm

BUVETTE
42 Grove Street (between Bedford and Bleecker), +1 212 255 3590
ilovebuvette.com, weekend brunch 10am – 4pm

DIM SUM GO GO
5 East Broadway (Kimlau Square), +1 212 732 0796
dimsumgogo.com, weekend brunch 10am – 10.30pm

HEARTH
403 East 12th Street (corner of 1st), +1 646 602 1300
restauranthearth.com, weekend brunch 11am – 2pm

ORIENTAL GARDEN
14 Elizabeth Street (between Bayard and Canal), +1 212 619 0085
orientalgardenny.com, open daily

THE BROOKLYN STAR
593 Lorimer Street (corner of Conselyea), +1 718 599 9899
thebrooklynstar.com, weekend brunch noon – 4pm

best brunches in nyc

Where weekenders recoup

Act 1: scene 1: After a night of debauchery, we awake to find ourselves clutching an aspirin bottle with regret lurking close by. Cut to the greasy, hearty, hair of the dog that is brunch. Grabbing a classic bodega egg, cheese and ham roll may seem S.O.P. in one's hangover cure regime, but in addition to the celebrated sandwiches at **Jacob's Pickles** (pg 67), **Rucola** (pg 76) and **LIC Market** (pg 115), here are a few storied specialty brunch alternatives.

At **Estela** (pg 32), the avocado, pancetta and egg sandwich is a sweet and savory concoction. Its poppy-seed bun, the Tebirke from local bakery Bien Cuit, consists of almond cream and a mix of Danish and croissant dough. As an alternative to **Buvette**'s delicious Nutella crepes or chicken salad, try their waffle sandwich – the combo of sunnyside egg, bacon and Gruyère topped with maple syrup has garnered a cult following. The quintessential meatloaf sandwich at **The Brooklyn Star**, served with a whimsical smiley face-shaped Sriracha sauce, can erase memories of any misdemeanors from the night prior. Between the apple cider donuts; five different Bloody Marys; local Finger Lakes yogurt and the pig trotter "Fiorentina", the choosing gets tough at **Hearth** so unleash your inner glutton and order everything.

For nonconformists, head to **Dim Sum Go Go** for creamy, pillowy dumplings. Although its décor may resemble an airport cafeteria, the food, such as their wispy, crisp spring rolls, is top-notch authentic fare. At **Oriental Garden**, dollies swim around the expansive, boisterous community tables offering fresh seafood and flaky egg-custard tarts. Vietnamese pho is traditionally served in the morning, and those who crave savory should head to **Ba Xuyên** for a salt fix with hot soup, an avocado shake, and a colossal bánh mì that costs less than $15 and can easily be shared.

soho

nolita, little italy, chinatown

In Chinatown, prepare to haggle over the price of everything from designer contact lenses to cigarettes – observe and learn from the grandmothers who queue for dried shrimp; or, if you want to step out of the fray and do some people watching, head to nearby Mott Street. Some may scoff and consider SoHo nothing but an overgrown, outdoor shopping mall and food court, yet this neighborhood remains a trendy area with majestic, cast iron structures. Whereas SoHo has expanded with major, international stores, Nolita, a neighborhood east of Bowery, is where you'll find local designers and small, independent shops, along Elizabeth and Mulberry Streets. Further east, Little Italy is slowly seeing a demographic shift: Chinatown businesses have sprouted further down Mulberry and Mott Streets, and the demand for linguine with clams is gradually giving way to hand-pulled noodles and Hoisin sauce.

1 Bánh Mì Saigon
2 Di Palo's Fine Foods
3 Estela
4 Love, Adorned
5 Michele Varian
6 Spicy Village (off map)
7 Thomas Sires
8 Warm

BÁNH MÌ SAIGON

Vietnamese on the go

198 Grand Street (between Mott and Mulberry) / **+1 212 941 1541**
banhmisaigonnyc.com / **Open daily**

In New York, skipping meals can quickly become the norm, especially
when stuck in a hectic work-driven environment. Soon, a Snickers bar and
coconut water from a bodega is considered a breakfast for champions. But
a quick meal can also be one much more worth eating. Bánh Mì Saigon is
a place where a five-dollar foot-long doesn't consist of corporate cold cuts.
Rather, flavorful warm meats such as barbecued pork and curried chicken
are enveloped inside fluffy French bread with a crackling crust. So, no
more excuses with the sugar-crash caprice: make way for a bánh mì with
a side order of thick, crunchy slabs of savory homemade shrimp chips.

DI PALO'S FINE FOODS

Italian specialty store

200 Grand Street (between Mott and Mulberry) / **+1 212 226 1033**
dipaloselects.com / **Open daily**

We had friends over for an impromptu dinner, and they brought meat and cheese to go with our wine, salad and bread. I had one slice of the mortadella, then another, and suddenly I was eyeing it sideways, trying to calculate how I could eat the rest without anyone noticing. The very next day, I got myself to Di Palo's for more. When a grocer has been around for more than 100 years and still has a line out of the door all day, you know they're doing something right. At Di Palo's that something is everything Italian — ricotta made daily, imported prosciutto and parmesan, and the best mortadella and provolone sandwiches ever. Take a queue number and use the wait to decide: smoked mozzarella, burrata, or both?

ESTELA

Sharable plates of culinary wonder

47 East Houston Street (between Mott and Mulberry)
+1 212 219 7693 / **estelanyc.com** / **Open daily**

Growing up in the Northwest, I had the opportune chance of befriending foragers who once invited me on an expedition. With a death grip around my hand-held GPS, the time spent in search for porcini mushrooms was a humbling experience — especially when returning home with only a handful of lowly grade no. 3's. The cuisine at Estela recalls such memories, as every pristine ingredient is like a hiding bolete or spectacular cilantro sauce waiting to be discovered. It's a beautiful environment where comfort meets precision. Chef Ignacio Mattos creates dishes meant for sharing, but after everyone's had their fair share you'll want to repeat the same order, reveling in the ephemeral flavors all by yourself.

LOVE, ADORNED
Artisan jewelry shop

169 Elizabeth Street (between Houston and Prince) / **+1 212 431 5683**
loveadorned.com / **Open daily**

My favorite nursery rhyme has always been the one about the fine lady atop a white horse with "rings on her fingers and bells on her toes". From that to my mother's armfuls of silver bangles, to the Persian necklaces I admired as a pre-teen on '70s singers, my definition of great jewelry is a little bohemian. Love, Adorned in Nolita has my number. The shop is a fantasy land, with trays and trays of gold and silver trinkets that are modern, a little bit country, and very rock and roll — detailed, very well made and not even a little precious. Pile it on and you're sure to have music wherever you go.

MICHELE VARIAN

Sleek Edwardian home décor

27 Howard Street (between Lafayette and Crosb
michelevarian.com / Open daily

Some say the best gifts often come in small packag
the best little knickknacks and home décor come in
importantly, always fits the bill, for homes of all size
designer cum boutique owner, sells handmade pillo
Edwardian times as well as tiny, ornate and playful t
anyone, even the hardened New Yorker who normall
Shui-ing the crap out of all items pre-purchase. Her v
she ingeniously sells in triple rolls, will enhance any
150 sq. feet or 4,500 sq. feet.

SPICY VILLAGE

Hole in the wall, Henan flavor

68 Forsyth Street (between Hester and Grand) / **+1 212 625 8299**
spicyvillageny.com / **Open daily**

The only way for me to describe my feelings about Spicy Village is through a love song: "My Spicy Village; Sweet comic Spicy Village; You make me smile with my heart. Your looks are laughable; Unphotographable; Yet you're my favorite plate of food. Is your décor less than Greek; Is your light a little weak? When I open the door to eat; Are you bright? But don't change a spice for me; (Plus, your price is right for me); I'll stay and eat noodles all day; Each day is Spicy Village day." My apologies to Sinatra, but there's no way his Valentine was as good as these hand-pulled Chinese noodles.

THOMAS SIRES

Gifts for mother and child

243 Elizabeth Street (between Houston and Prince)
+1 646 692 4472 / thomassires.com / Open daily

It seems that one always finds more items in your personal shopping basket than in the one for others, while scouting for those last-minute gifts. At Thomas Sires you can fill both. Owners Fiona Thomas and Allison Sires cleverly curate their store displays with the most darling mementos, beautifully designed ready-to-wear pieces, and cute onesies for newborns and toddlers. From silk dresses composed of modern prints to rolls of tear-by-the-piece handkerchiefs made from pure cotton, you can walk away with a gift for you, me and everyone you know. So go ahead, justify an early birthday present and treat yourself.

WARM

Surf style for the City

181 Mott Street (between Kenmare and Broome) / +1 212 925 1200
warmny.com   Open daily

Imagine you're at the beach: you throw on a flimsy dress over your favorite crocheted bikini, smooth on some coconut oil, and slip your toes into embroidered huaraches. On your way out the door, you grab a woven bag stuffed with a colorful shawl and a good book, as well as your daughter's favorite sundress and stuffed animal. OK, now imagine all the same things, only instead of walking out onto sand, you're in the middle of New York. Feels a lot easier to face the city now, right? And surely there's a rooftop pool waiting for you somewhere. At Warm, island life is a moveable feast, and they've got all the goods to make the urban jungle your personal paradise.

BARGEMUSIC
Fulton Ferry Landing, +1 718 624 4924, bargemusic.org

BIRDLAND
315 West 44th Street (between 8th and 9th), +1 212 581 3080
birdlandjazz.com

CAMEO GALLERY
93 North 6th Street (between Wythe and Berry), +1 718 302 1180
cameony.com

GLASSLANDS GALLERY
289 Kent Avenue (between South 1st and South 2nd)
theglasslands.com

(LE) POISSON ROUGE
158 Bleecker Street (corner of Thompson), +1 212 505 3474
lepoissonrouge.com

MERCURY LOUNGE
217 East Houston (corner of Essex), +1 212 260 4700
mercuryloungenyc.com

PIANOS
158 Ludlow Street (corner of Stanton), +1 212 505 3733
pianosnyc.com

ROCKWOOD MUSIC HALL
196 Allen Street (between East Houston and Stanton)
+1 212 477 4155, rockwoodmusichall.com

SMALLS JAZZ CLUB
183 West 10th Street (corner of 7th), smallsjazzclub.com

THE BOWERY BALLROOM
6 Delancey (between Bowery and Chrystie), +1 212 533 2111
boweryballroom.com

VILLAGE VANGUARD
178 7th Avenue South (corner of Waverly), +1 212 255 4037
villagevanguard.com

Check websites for all show times

live entertainment

The Carnegie Hall alternative

Be they divas looking to become the next Aretha or a new band whose sole release has just gone viral, NY is an epicenter for aspiring musicians. Those who've already made it might insist on performing on the hallowed stages of Madison Square Garden or Barclays Center, but if you're interested in catching the next-big-thing-before-they-get-big, then shimmy your way to these venues.

Historical landmark **The Bowery Ballroom** still boasts some of its original 1930s fittings but there's nothing dated about the acoustics – the sound quality is the big draw for both performers and fans alike. The **Mercury Lounge** has been a launchpad for many a rocker, including the Yeah Yeah Yeahs who made their debut here in 2000. Singer-songwriters to rock bands are regularly discovered on one of the stages at cover-charge-free **Rockwood Music Hall**, while those with a more indie bent flock to **Pianos**, where multiple shows are performed simultaneously in this bar, restaurant and dance club.

For everything from contemporary classical to the avant-garde, visit **(Le) Poisson Rouge**, a multimedia venue founded by musicians from the Manhattan School of Music. Alternatively, **Glasslands Gallery**, a warehouse converted into a sound stage, offers an intimate and psychedelic experience, whereas **Cameo Gallery**, an art space and restaurant, turns the spotlight on comedians and indie and electronic musicians.

Beyond the halls of Carnegie and Alice Tully, classical music enthusiasts can enjoy concerts in **Bargemusic**, where a floating barge takes center stage and the East River and lower Manhattan skyline act as backdrop.

Jazz is synonymous with New York, and iconic spots such as **Birdland** echo the syncopated beats from the days of Charlie Parker and Dixieland blues. At **Smalls Jazz Club**, the 60 seats fill up fast but don't worry – all performances are streamed live. And finally, dubbed the Carnegie Hall of jazz, thanks to headline acts that include John Coltrane and Dexter Gordon, the **Village Vanguard** has had audiences swoonin' and swingin' for nearly 80 years.

chelsea and greenwich village

meatpacking, west village

Home to many art dealers, opening evenings see art aficionados parading through galleries, clinking flutes with fellow enthusiasts and scrutinizing the latest shows. Summertime attracts picnickers here, as Chelsea Market in the Meatpacking district offers fresh, steamed lobster to nibble on in the High Line park, where manicured grass awaits, with a view of the Hudson. Before or after lunching al fresco, shop to your heart's content at the many high-end and independent designer shops in the neighborhood. Or, hit the cobblestoned streets of Greenwich Village to explore the small boutiques and quaint cafés. A few more steps toward the West Village and you'll discover a labyrinth of hidden gems along Cornelia Street.

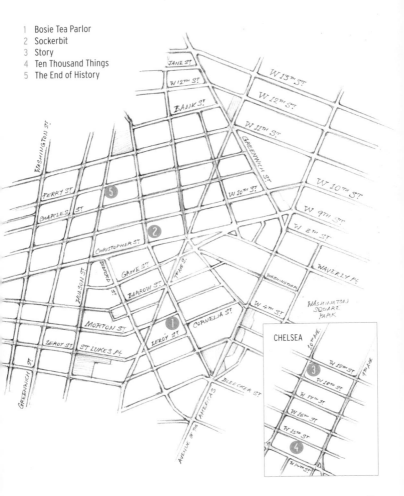

1 Bosie Tea Parlor
2 Sockerbit
3 Story
4 Ten Thousand Things
5 The End of History

CHELSEA

41

BOSIE TEA PARLOR

Afternoon refreshment and treats

10 Morton Street (between 7th and Bleecker) / +1 212 352 9900
bosienyc.com / Open daily

Take a French, fourth-generation pastry chef, put him in a cozy gem of a West Village space, add an extensive tea collection, and voilà: a winning result. Bosie is a cool haven in the summer, when a matcha green tea éclair is just the right sweet treat. In snowstorms, a mug of almond tea and the best canelé in town warm me to my toes. When guests are in town, I insist on taking them here for the tea service that comes complete with mini cucumber and egg salad sandwiches (crusts removed, naturally). If you go, give me a nod; I'll be the girl in the corner ogling a pile of pastry.

SOCKERBIT

Swedish imports and specialty licorice

89 Christopher Street (between Bleecker and West 4th)
+1 212 206 8170 / sockerbit.com / Open daily

My dentist once facetiously censured my guilty pleasure diet (e.g., potato chips and licorice) stating that I possessed the dental record of an 80-year-old before nonchalantly acquainting me with my retribution. Sockerbit, meaning "sugar cube", is a Scandinavian candy store in the Village that sells sweets by the pound. Carrying 150 different types of candy flavors, many sans artificial flavoring, they also offer imports such as lingonberry jam and elderflower syrup. This may be a dentist's worst nightmare, but to the incorrigible sweet tooth it warrants extra candy in one hand and dental floss in the other.

STORY

Virtual magazine meets retail

144 10th Street (corner of 19th) / **+1 212 242 4853** / thisisstory.com
Closed Monday

If one could ever physically walk along the lines and sidebars of a print magazine, Story would be the place to do it. Not only does it house a gallery, but also the editorial writings on the wall, it stocks local merchandise and it practices philanthropy. This ambidextrous retail store can be mistaken for a "pop-up" shop, but between Story's printed words there's a longer tale to tell. Owner Rachel Shechtman has curated 12 different themes since Story's launch, all of which read like an art exhibition, editorial calendar and community outreach program rolled into one.

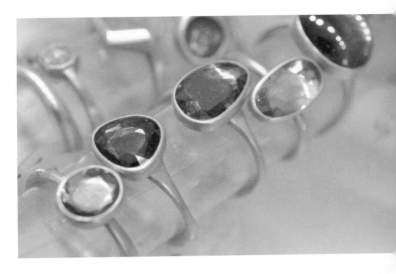

TEN THOUSAND THINGS

Modern classic jewelry

423 West 14th Street (between 8th and 9th) / +1 212 352 1333
tenthousandthings.com / Open daily

It would be no surprise if King Midas had touched the Redwood Forest
and the precious metals of organic foliage had drifted into the jewelry
cases at Ten Thousand Things. Co-owners and designers David Rees
and Ron Anderson designed their first range in 1991. Their selection is
gleaned from the traditions of heirloom pieces and refined intricacies.
Other local artists who share the same philosophy of modern delicacy
are showcased within the warm, birch-wood-walled gallery. I discovered
my first TTT treasure over ten years ago and it remains my most
complimented possession to this day. Nature's beauty in jewelry form is
simply priceless.

THE END OF HISTORY

World's largest array of vintage glass

548 1/2 Hudson Street (between Perry and Charles)
+1 212 647 7598 / **theendofhistoryshop.blogspot.com** / **Open daily**

Walking into this compact showroom of delicate collectables prompts the fear of turning into that accident-prone caricature who shatters everything in sight. But not to worry, because owner Stephen Saunders makes great use of the limited shelving space, carefully displaying obscure pieces such as French opaline apothecary jars, Italian glass urns, and hand-cut porcelain vases. With its specialty in vintage hand-blown glass, ceramics and porcelain housewares, what's old is new again at The End of History. There's nothing like traveling back in time and imagining past interiors in which these elegant pieces once resided. It makes one want to dismiss today's disposable-everything and possess such treasures once again.

NYC AFTER DARK
clandestine cocktail bars

ATTABOY

Here in New York, seasoned barkeeps present cocktail menus as long as novellas, and readers pine for sequels. Camaraderie keeps the industry uninhibited and the so-called bartender crush means the pros enthusiastically swap recipes and concepts over mixed drinks (or a surreptitious, ahem, beer).

Industry pioneer Sasha Petraske of **Milk & Honey** continues to whet one's curiosity, but with today's fixation on the niche the list of specialty bars has grown exponentially. Carrying over 200 single-malt whiskies, head over to **Keen's Steakhouse** for a scotch or few, and the atmosphere will take you back to its established date of 1885.

Or if you see yourself as a Chartreuse connoisseur, head to **Pouring Ribbons** on Avenue C – it stocks vintage liquors dating back to the 1940s. Bittersweet palates can enjoy over 50 amari and digestifs at the handsome tile bar inside **Amor y Amargo**, while those seeking a weekend brunch-time hair of the dog will find solace in the double buzz of an amaro cocktail paired with rich pour-over coffee.

Cocktail veterans David Kaplan, Alex Day and Natasha David run **Nitecap**, a dimly lit hideaway where local luminary barkeeps mix innovative and potent elixirs, alongside an extensive brandy list.

Attaboy, a prohibition-era style saloon, is located south of Delancey; much quieter territory compared to inebriated Lower East Side dive bars. Former Milk & Honey barkeeps, Sam Ross and Michael McIlroy, have the uncanny skill of prescribing the tastiest bespoke drinks with chemist precision. There, the push of a discreet bell opens the door to rousing cocktails and handwritten tabs. Further downtown, drop by **The Dead Rabbit**, an expansive two-floor taproom that specializes in Nogs, Smashes and other 19th-century concoctions.

Brooklyn bars offer just as tasty mixology, but nothing beats an inviting patio space like **Weather Up** in Prospect Heights. In Williamsburg, find comfort that genuine, friendly service still exists alongside an impressive bourbon selection at **Post Office**. In Queens, two words: **Dutch Kills**.

AMOR Y AMARGO

AMOR Y AMARGO
443 East 6th Street (corner of Avenue A), +1 212 614 6818
amoryamargony.com, open daily

ATTABOY
134 East Eldridge Street (corner of Broome), no website, open daily

DUTCH KILLS
27-24 Jackson Avenue (between Dutch Kills and Queens), +1 718 383 2724
dutchkillsbar.com, open daily

KEENS STEAKHOUSE
72 West 36th Street (between 5th and 6th), +1 212 947 3636, keens.com
open daily

MILK & HONEY
30 East 23rd Avenue (between Broadway and Park), mlkhny.com, open daily

NITECAP
120 Rivington Street (downstairs basement; between Essex and
Norfolk), +1 212 466 3361, nitecapnyc.com, open daily

POST OFFICE
188 Havemeyer Street (corner of South 4th), +1 718 963 2574
postofficebk.com, closed Sunday

POURING RIBBONS
225 Avenue B (2nd Floor; between East 13th and 14th), +1 917 656 6788
pouringribbons.com, open daily

THE DEAD RABBIT
30 Water Street (corner of Broad), +1 646 422 7906
deadrabbitnyc.com, open daily

WEATHER UP
589 Vanderbilt Avenue (between Dean and Bergen)
weatherupnyc.com, open daily

BENKAI RAMEN (inside USHIWAKAMARU)
136 West Houston Street (between Thompson and Macdougal)
+1 212 228 4181, ushiwakamarunyc.com, closed Sunday and Monday

BUVETTE
42 Grove Street (between Bedford and Bleecker), +1 212 255 3590
ilovebuvette.com, open daily

GREAT NY NOODLETOWN
28 Bowery (between Bayard and Pell), +1 212 349 0923
greatnynoodletown.com, open daily

PUNJABI GROCERY & DELI
114 East 1st Street (between A and 1st), +1 212 533 3356
no website, open daily

SOUTH BROOKLYN PIZZA
122 1st Avenue (between St Marks and East 7th), +1 212 533 2879
southbrooklynpizza.com, open daily

TACO MORELOS
Avenue A (corner of 3rd), +1 347 772 5216, no website, open daily

TERRIOR WINE BAR
413 East 12th Street (between A and 1st), +1 646 602 1300
restauranthearth.com/terrior, open daily

THE REDHEAD
349 East 13th Street (between 1st and 2nd), +1 212 533 6212
theredheadnyc, open daily

WO-HOP
15 Mott Street, +1 212 566 3841, wohopnyc.com, open daily

NYC AFTER DARK
nocturnal supper spots

New York City has many hidden gems for those still on the prowl long after everyone else has called it a night. At 1am, Michelin-starred service staff zombie-walk toward East Village for post-shift imbibes, house-cured duck breast at **Terrior Wine Bar**, or juicy fried chicken at **The Redhead**. Across Tompkins Square Park, **Maiden Lane** (pg 17), a beloved neighborhood seafood-centric gastropub serves magnificent shrimp and lobster rolls. For a Sicilian slice – or four – head to **South Brooklyn Pizza**. The venerable 24-hour taqueria **Taco Morelos** is known to serve its tender tacos *al suadero* (a thin, smooth-textured cut of beef) until sunrise. Cab drivers jumpstart 4am shifts with lentils and samosas at **Punjabi Grocery & Deli**.

If sifting through countless Japanese izakayas on Saint Marks in the East Village makes one woozy, head to West Village's celebrated sushi restaurant **Ushiwakamaru**, where nocturnal pop-up **Benkai Ramen** serves noodles Tuesday through Saturday, after the sushi counter shuts down. Francophiles rejoice, for crispy Forestiers filled with layers of mushrooms and Gruyère are at **Buvette**, and the croque-monsieur variation is available until 2am.

Celebrity chef sightings have commonly taken place into the wee morning hours at **Great NY Noodletown** in Chinatown, where an aromatic bowl of wonton noodle soup can be found on practically every table. The chef who switches rotation right on the midnight hour to prepare perfectly steamed fish and succulent snails at one of Chinatown's last remaining 24-hour restaurants, **Wo-Hop**, boggles even sober minds. There's only one kitchen here, but the staff refer to the downstairs seating as "Americanized" whereas upstairs, the authenticity is found on the whole head of a flounder. Take heed.

midtown west and midtown east

union square, flatiron, gramercy, hell's kitchen

Midtown West includes neighborhoods such as Hell's Kitchen, Theater District and Times Square. Moling through Penn Station can be overwhelming, and negotiating 8th and 9th Avenues can often feel like walking through Middle America on stilts, squeezing past balloon-sized, corporate fast food chains. In 2015, Times Square's iconic jumbotron will be replaced by a 24,000-square-foot LED screen. New York just wouldn't be the same without the juxtaposition found in Theater District of an Off-Broadway musical and a hole in the wall eatery. Murray Hill in Midtown East is largely residential, neighboring landmarks such as the Empire State Building, Grand Central Station and Bryant Park. Korea Way, west of Murray Hill, is a street with nocturnal electric energy, and home to 24-hour karaoke bars, Korean barbecue restaurants and regrettable soju intoxication (you've been warned).

1 Café China
2 Corkbuzz Wine Studio (off map)
3 Gazala's Place
4 Metalliferous
5 Nepenthes
6 Pastrami Queen (off map)
7 Tehuitzingo Mexican Deli & Taqueria
8 Tiffin Wallah

MIDTOWN EAST

CAFÉ CHINA

Sichuan cuisine in 1930s Shanghai setting

13 East 37th Street (between 4th and 5th) / +1 212 213 2810
cafechinanyc.com / Open daily

Chinese expats Xian Zhang and his wife Yiming Wang understand the transportive abilities of a restaurant. At Café China, the magic happens before the first bite. From the moment you sidle up to the mirrored Art Deco bar and order a cocktail by the name of Lust/Caution, you're in their version of glamorous pre-war Shanghai. The drinks and atmosphere are stylish enough for this to be solely a cocktail destination, but it would be a crime to miss the food. It's Sichuan to be reckoned with: riotous flavors, numbing peppercorns, and a mapo tofu that rivals any other. In the snarl of Midtown East, Café China is nothing short of a miracle.

CORKBUZZ WINE STUDIO

Wine classes for the curious oenophile

13 East 13th Street (between 5th and 13th) / +1 646 873 6071
corkbuzz.com / Open daily

Corkbuzz wine classes seem to be the place where wine novices earn their GED's and oenophiles their doctorates, as tastings may vary from an uncomplicated Sancerre to a '61 Petrus. It's a place to drink, listen and savor the harmonious marriage of Master Sommelier Laura Maniec's precise wine pairings with Chef Hayan Yi's delicacies. Two lessons ring true of the 27 curriculums offered. There's no right or wrong pairing. Here, imbibers' perception of taste is changed, discovering why steak tartar pairs splendidly with a glass of Viura. Lesson number two? Snootiness inhibits stuck-up noses from smelling accurately. Lessons duly noted.

GAZALA'S PLACE

Druze cuisine from the motherland

709 9th Avenue (between 48th and 49th) / +1 212 245 0709
gazalasplace.com / Open daily

Gazala's Place, one of those classic New York hallway restaurants, is short on space but its food is so delicious that it occupies a huge piece of real estate in my pantheon of eateries. It's also one of those uber-regional specialists that introduced me to the subtle difference between "Middle Eastern" general and Druze cuisine specifically. Druze food is all about flatbread, not to be confused with pita. Bowls of hummus, labneh (strained goats' milk yogurt cheese) dusted with *za'atar* spice, fish grilled whole with lemon: all are best eaten with pieces ripped from the large, thin rounds of fermented bread served warm when you sit down. As you leave, don't forget to buy a börek or five for lunch tomorrow; you won't be sorry.

METALLIFEROUS

Ultimate jewelry supply

3rd Floor, 34 West 46th Street (between 5th and 6th)
+1 212 944 0909 / metalliferous.com / Closed Saturday and Sunday

As a delusional eight-year-old I thought I could pull a Steve Jobs at my parents' yard sale selling handmade jewelry. Unfortunately my octogenarian neighbors didn't exchange their social security nickels for my florescent-beaded earrings. I may have misinterpreted my cash flow forecast, but I regret more so that a Metalliferous didn't exist in my cul-de-sac. This small store carries over 30,000 base metal materials, new and vintage beads, and tools. It is the one-stop shop where sculptors, jewelry designers and novice hobbyists come to gather what they need to make their art. Time to reopen the jewelry stand...

NEPENTHES

Americana craftsmanship meets Japanese design

307 West 38th Street (between 8th and 9th) / +1 212 643 9540
nepenthesny.com / Open daily

Against the cacophony within the concrete canyon of Hell's Kitchen, Nepenthes stands cooly like a quiet wallflower. Its name carries two meanings: the literal Japanese translation is what manager Abdul Abasi describes as "a drug that cures all woes". The homonym is the name of a carnivorous plant. Both meanings elicit truth. Much like for the prey lured by a Venus flytrap's pheromone, once you enter it's difficult to leave. The showroom itself could cure the deepest melancholia. Engineered Garments, the Japanese-based brand stocked at Nepenthes, is made in NYC's Garment District. Even the most discerning shopper will admire the industrious, strong seams, and be reminded of what "Made-in-America" once stood for.

PASTRAMI QUEEN

Sandwich royalty

1125 Lexington Avenue (corner of 78th) / **+1 212 734 1500**
pastramiqueen.com / **Open daily**

Like the Empire State Building, Central Park and angry taxi drivers, some
things just belong to NYC. My favorite icon? Pastrami on thin-sliced rye
with lots of mustard, and no one does it better than the Queen. Sure,
there are other places more famous, but the first time I bit into the huge,
meltingly fatty specimen here, I pledged my allegiance to this sandwich
and I've never had reason to question that in all the years since. Yet, if
perfect pastrami isn't enough for you, here's the bonus round: the matzoh
ball soup will cure what ails you, and then some.

EHUITZINGO MEXICAN
ELI & TAQUERIA

joint in the back of a bodega

10th Avenue (between 47th and 48th)   +1 212 397 5956
tzingo.net / Open daily

d about Tehuitzingo long before I set foot in it, only no one could
nber the name. "Have you been to that taco spot in the bodega?"
ne asked. Others mentioned vaguely "the best Mexican in the city,
10th". The last straw was when I smelled delicious food coming
e office next to mine, and begged to know where they got it: "you
hat weird taco place in the grocery store." Some next-level Googling
to the best goat tacos this side of the border – and yes, it's hidden
Mexican grocery, so you can pick up other goodies for later.

TIFFIN WALLAH

Bombay-style vegetarian cuisine

127 East 28th Street (between Park and Lexington) / **+1 212 685 7301**
tiffindelivery.us / **Open daily**

I'm a bit wary of buffets – too often the food is coagulated in the chafing tray and smells suspiciously like airplane food. I don't mean to sound hoity-toity, but an all-you-can-eat special can be like playing Russian roulette, where the loser wins food poisoning. Lunch at Tiffin Wallah, on the other hand, is far from this paranoid misconception. Helpful servers peek over diner's shoulders and offer ten different condiments for a chapati. The always smiling head chef, Y.N. Moortho, stands proudly behind his trays of fragrant, Bombay style cuisine. My only concern is whether he has replenished the depleted dosas by the time I'm ready for that third helping.

upper west side
and
upper east side

harlem, morningside heights

Historic for its music culture, the Upper West Side begins near Columbus Circle, cradling Central Park from West 59th to 110th Street. John Lennon devotees visit the Strawberry Fields Memorial across from his former home, and at Lincoln Center, luxurious meals satiate those donning opera gloves or ostentatious outfits during Fashion Week. The Upper East Side has a prim and restrained scene – the dogs being walked seem to pick up after themselves. Beaux-Arts-style mansions, with built-in elevators, pipe all along Madison Avenue. East of Central Park, The Neue Gallery, The Metropolitan Museum, and the Guggenheim showcase some of the world's greatest art. West of Lenox Avenue, live Puerto Rican music echoes from Spanish Harlem (a.k.a. El Barrio) and locals flock for juicy fried chicken and old jazz standards in Harlem proper. Despite the venerable Lenox Lounge closure and recent sprouting of corporate suburbia, Harlem maintains its heritage of Renaissance Revival architecture and obligatory Sunday brunch.

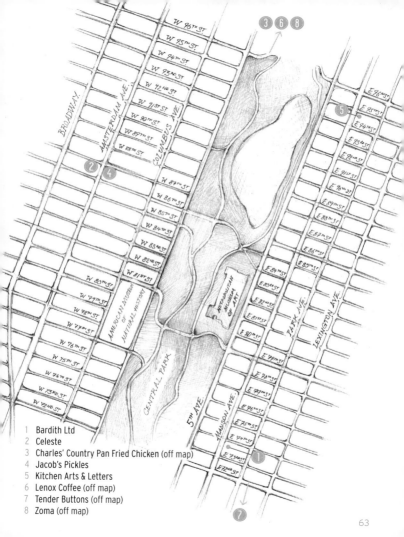

1 Bardith Ltd
2 Celeste
3 Charles' Country Pan Fried Chicken (off map)
4 Jacob's Pickles
5 Kitchen Arts & Letters
6 Lenox Coffee (off map)
7 Tender Buttons (off map)
8 Zoma (off map)

63

BARDITH LTD

18th-century English porcelain and pottery

901 Madison Avenue (between 72nd and 73rd) / **+1 212 737 3775**
bardith.com / **Closed Sunday**

Feeling like the quite literal bull in a china shop, I spent a few minutes in Bardith Ltd terrified I would break everything, until I relaxed and started really seeing what was on the closely packed shelves around me. More museum than shop, the china spans centuries and continents, all of the quality that can make an antiques lover weep. They ship all over the world to collectors, but if you don't have hundreds to spend on exquisite examples of British bone china, it's a treasure trove for inspiration alone. Whether you're a clothing designer, illustrator, or just plain interested, the intricate patterns and unusual color palettes are sure to play muse to your inner artist.

CELESTE

Little Naples in the city

502 Amsterdam Avenue (between 84th and 85th) / **+1 212 874 4559**
celestenewyork.com / **Open daily**

Walking into Celeste feels like returning to an old friend's dining room. Owner Carmine, with his towering height and stoic demeanor, welcomes the line of regulars by a nod of approval. Celeste shares Neapolitan-style home cooking using minimal, fresh ingredients. This includes an impressive menu of obscure Italian cheeses. Listen carefully as Carmine recites the list at gunshot speed, offering an extensive flavor profile and bovine history for each. The aroma of sautéed mussels and pan-seared chicken livers makes it difficult to stick to the original intention of ordering a stellar hand-tossed, wood-fired pizza. After one visit you'll want to return, knowing you'll probably get a venerable nod along with your satisfied stomach.

CHARLES' COUNTRY PAN FRIED CHICKEN

Harlem's soul-food fry master

2839 Frederick Douglass Boulevard (between West 151st and 152nd)
+1 212 281 1800 / No website / Open daily

I'd like to think the average New Yorker avoids triple-transfer train rides — especially when only in search of fried chicken. Having said that, Charles' Country Pan Fried Chicken up in Harlem is my favorite mom and pop fry house, even with its harshly lit, foil-lined deli case that's always nearly empty. That's because Chef Charles Gabriel's egg-washed, flour-dredged chicken is pan-fried in small batches in the gargantuan cast iron pan. It would be absurd to endure the train ride home before devouring the crispy chicken "to-go" so I always eat-in. Let's just say the chicken is so good, I don't mind my fellow commuters casting glances at the juice stains that inevitably end up on my clothes.

JACOB'S PICKLES

Comfort food for night owls

509 Amsterdam Avenue (between 84th and 85th) / **+1 212 470 5566**
jacobspickles.com / **Open daily**

Everyone knows NYC never sleeps. But Jacob's Pickles is a real soul-food gem for night owls. Here, waiters graciously plate up toothsome brine-based comfort food until 4am, for weary service industry folk and the young office crowd alike. Owner Jacob Hadjigeorgis is passionate about his craft. Delicate flights of crisp pickles are treated as if plating caviar. White Lily flour is shipped from the South to make sure the biscuits meet texture standards. Marvelous microbrews are always on tap. A distinguished balance in acidity, sweetness and richness makes it almost too easy to forget about personal food hang-ups: it never takes long to find a way to rationalize that order of deep-fried Oreos.

KITCHEN ARTS & LETTERS

New and out-of-print cookbooks

1435 Lexington Avenue (between East 93rd and 94th)
+1 212 876 5550 / kitchenartsandletters.com
Closed Sunday (also closed Saturdays in July and August)

Admittedly, buying a copy of Yann Duytsche's *Sweet Diversions* when I possess only a manual whisk is akin to buying $1,200 Christian Louboutin's when training for a triathlon. But like shoes, there are some things a girl has to have. Depending on tastes and cooking know-how, staff at Kitchen Arts & Letters (who are more like seasoned librarians), prescribe the best books of culinary lore. Catalogued by subject, there are even copies of niche periodicals, such as *FOOL* from Sweden and *Apicius* from Spain, in limited numbers. So whether you want to learn Medieval Arab cookery or revisit Elizabeth David's memoir, you'll find the perfect recipe to satiate any kitchen curiosity.

LENOX COFFEE

A community hangout serving great java

60 West 129th Street (between Lenox and 5th) / **+1 646 833 7839**
lenoxcoffee.com / **Open daily**

During the years I've lived in New York, I've seen coffee culture go from Greek deli takeout to Blue Bottle Chemex. Is there anything better than hanging out all day over a latte and thick slab of banana bread, and chatting up fellow patrons about the new hat shop down the street? That's a rhetorical question, and the answer is no. Lucky for me, now that Lenox Coffee is here, so is coffee shop culture. Not only are the baristas skilled, but they will start conversations with you while you wait! Plus, the coffee is great, and with its queue of locals and regulars it'll only be a matter of time before this place becomes an institution. We've come a long way, baby.

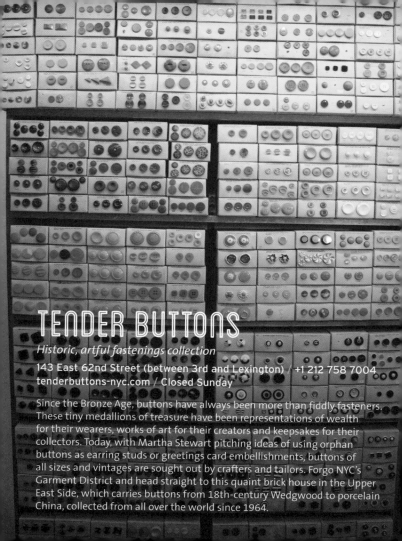

TENDER BUTTONS

Historic, artful fastenings collection

143 East 62nd Street (between 3rd and Lexington) / +1 212 758 7004
tenderbuttons-nyc.com / Closed Sunday

Since the Bronze Age, buttons have always been more than fiddly fasteners.
These tiny medallions of treasure have been representations of wealth
for their wearers, works of art for their creators and keepsakes for their
collectors. Today, with Martha Stewart pitching ideas of using orphan
buttons as earring studs or greetings card embellishments, buttons of
all sizes and vintages are sought out by crafters and tailors. Forgo NYC's
Garment District and head straight to this quaint brick house in the Upper
East Side, which carries buttons from 18th-century Wedgwood to porcelain
China, collected from all over the world since 1964.

ZOMA

Bright and fresh Ethiopian cuisine

2084 Frederick Douglas Boulevard (corner of 113th)
+1 212 662 0620 / zomanyc.com / Open daily

There's a scene in an episode of *The Simpsons* where Marge tries Ethiopian food for the first time, with great trepidation. The flavors transform her tongue into a disco-floor, complete with a glitter ball, Ethiopian music and trippy Marge-shaped dancing taste buds. Watching, I immediately craved a huge platter of berbere-spiced lentils and turmeric-dyed veggies. So, I decided to make the trek up to Harlem for Zoma. I can't claim to be an expert on injera (sourdough flatbread) or doro wat (a chicken curry), but there was definitely dancing in my mouth, which I complemented with a big glass of honey wine. And just like that Simpsons episode, there was enough food for leftovers. Art inspires life, indeed.

red hook and gowanus

boerum hill, carroll gardens

You've got to admire the tenacity of the residents and business owners of these South Brooklyn neighborhoods, who rebuilt their lives after the battering 13-foot-high waves unleashed by Hurricane Sandy in 2012. Red Hook, named for the color of its soil, is best visited by water taxi, which allows for picture perfect skyline views including, of course, the lady herself, The Statue of Liberty. Eastward is Gowanus, a neighborhood known for its industrial setting and alleged mobster-related corpses that purportedly float in the Gowanus Canal. Despite the grisly allegations, the serene residential nooks along Smith Street and charming eateries along 3rd Avenue are definitely not to be missed.

1 El Olomega
2 Littleneck
3 Rucola
4 Shelsky's Smoked Fish
5 The Brooklyn Circus
6 Twig Terrariums

EL OLOMEGA

Little El Salvador in a food truck

155 Bay Street (corner of Clinton) / **elolomega.com**
Open daily, May to October (and some weekends in December)

The Lainez family pupusas (stuffed tortillas) truck operates from their coveted corner at Clinton and Bay Street, their base since 1990. There's no other food truck that has served locals for this long in Red Hook Park. This family-owned Salvadorian pupuseria makes their corn tortillas from additive-free maseca flour and their fillings of pork, chicken, cheese or veggies, including spinach, beans and sweet plantain, in small batches. Silvia Ceron, one of six women inside what appears to be a retired school bus, stands aside a blazing-hot, five-foot griddle, feverishly whipping up delights such as curtido, a bright red cabbage slaw that has such incredible tang, it practically razor-cuts through the creamy pockets of gooey cheese.

LITTLENECK

Lobster rolls for the seafarer

288 3rd Avenue (between President and Carroll) / +1 718 522 1921
littleneckbrooklyn.com / Closed Tuesday

If there was ever a lobster roll eating contest, I'd walk home with a dozen blue ribbons — especially if it were held at Littleneck. The lobster here has just the right amount of aioli, zing and sweetness, all enveloped in a little buttery bun that stays crisp to the last bite of juicy meat. The restaurant surrounds seafood lovers with a quaint nautical theme that evokes the scent of New England's sea air. Perhaps the competition comes at the end of the seafood feast, in seeing who has enough room left to do justice to a slice of locally made pie from The Blue Stove bakery.

RUCOLA

Northern Italian farm to table

190 Dean Street (corner of Bond) / **+1 718 576 3209**
rucolabrooklyn.com / **Open daily**

Tucked away inside a handsome corner brownstone, Rucola's diners
gravitate to its center communal table and are transported to a pastoral
Piemonte scene, where aromas of fresh herbs and white truffles dominate.
It's the ultimate neighborhood gem, serving up bountiful grilled goodies
and taking every opportunity to turn a simple gathering into a joyous
celebration. To find this centerpiece of old-world Italian in historic Brooklyn,
look out for its romantic wrought-iron façade with a prolific array of
verdant foliage.

SHELSKY'S SMOKED FISH

Old-school Jewish delicatessen

251 Smith Street (between Douglass and Degraw)
+1 718 855 8817 / shelskys.com / Closed Monday

I once lived on the West coast and deemed it "best coast" due to its abundance of fresh, Pacific seafood. But when it comes to cured fish, New York reigns legendary. Owner Peter Shelsky keeps it local, carrying produce from Brooklyn's cure kings ACME Smoked Fish and The Smokehouse in Mamaroneck, while bagels and bialys come from Lower East Side's Kossar's and Davidivitch in Queens. What better bagels to envelope layers of silky lox and smooth, dense cream cheese? Peter's very own whitefish salad, folded together with rich mayonnaise and crunchy, house-pickled cucumbers, is so addictive, just pray there's room in your carry-on to show West coasters what's up.

THE BROOKLYN CIRCUS

Vintage Americana

150 Nevins Street (between Bergen and Wyckoff) / +1 718 858 0919
thebkcircus.com / Closed Monday

Lauded as being a fashion visionary, store-owner Ouigi Theodore has
proven that looking back to the past is a way of moving forward in fashion.
Whether it's the Harlem Renaissance or the Civil Rights Movement, fashion
finds references from history's landscape. Ouigi's inspirations range from
his Haitian roots, to NYC culture, Marcus Garvey and *The Cosby Show*, and
these are all incorporated into the store's emphasis on vintage. Having
grown up playing baseball and varsity football, a strong collegiate, athletic
slant can be seen in his sportswear and expertly tailored casual clothes.
With fashion always evolving, Ouigi's philosophy of a constant editing
eye for reinvention is what has allowed The Brooklyn Circus to transcend

TWIG TERRARIUMS

Little worlds of wonder

287 3rd Avenue (between President and Carroll) / +1 718 488 8944
twigterrariums.com / Closed Monday–Wednesday

Perhaps it was *Gulliver's Travels* that tickled my imagination for pocket-sized wonderment. Or perhaps it is living in a claustrophobic tenement abode that has made me a lover of little things. My miniature stove; tiny settee; a brawny Douglas Fir branch-turned-Christmas-tree all create an illusion that enlarges my small surroundings. At Twig Terrariums, co-owners Katy Maslow and Michelle Inciarrano custom design microscopically detailed terrariums for closeted tree-hugging New Yorkers. Scenes range from nature hikes through manicured trails to salty scenes of licentious exhibitionists within unruly, lush moss. Commissions, however excruciatingly painstaking, such as hand-painting specific hair color on figurines, are welcome.

graffiti masterpieces

NY's vivid storytellers

Its ink may seem permanent, but NY street art is transient. Whether it's the cryptic epigrams of SAMO© artist and Warhol-collaborator Jean-Michel Basquiat in the L.E.S.; Cost & Revs's obscure wheat-pasting exploits; or crochet street artist Olek; graffiti inevitably gets replaced with at best, something equally inspired or at worst, by gentrified high-rise condos.

Thankfully, countless legendary local and international artists continue to voice out and transform dilapidated brick walls into colorful manifestos. Head east from Williamsburg to find **The Bushwick Collective**, an outdoor gallery in an industrial warehouse area. It sustains the now defunct 5Pointz Aerosol Art Center's philosophy of uniting street artists from NY's five boroughs with their brethren all over the world. You'll see signature styles from locals, such as Joe Lurato, Buff Monster and Jerkface here.

In Manhattan, 5Pointz founder Jonathan Cohen, a.k.a. Meres One, has found a new canvas on **Rag & Bone's Wall** in Nolita. Over at Houston and Bowery, **The Bowery Mural**, the spot that once hosted Keith Haring's famous mural in 1982 has turned into a sanctioned outdoor exhibition space that is constantly updated with new works from different artists.

Two original **Keith Haring** exterior murals remain today, one at the Carmine outdoor swimming pool in Greenwich Village and the other in East Harlem. While near East Harlem, make sure to also check out the latest paintings at **Graffiti Hall of Fame**. Back in Chelsea, their oversized cousins tower over **The High Line**, from where you can see changing pieces commissioned throughout the year.

5POINTZ STREET ART AT RAG & BONE'S WALL
East Houston and Elizabeth Street

GRAFFITI HALL OF FAME
East 106th Street and Park Avenue

KEITH HARING EXTERIOR MURALS
Carmine Street Mural, 1987; Carmine Street and 7th Avenue; Crack is Wack, 1986; East 128th Street and 2nd Avenue by FDR Drive

THE BOWERY MURAL
Houston and Bowery Street

THE BUSHWICK COLLECTIVE
Troutman Street and Saint Nicholas Avenue, Bushwick, Brooklyn

THE HIGH LINE STREET ART
529 West 20th Street

THE BUSHWICK COLLECTIVE

fort greene and prospect heights

dumbo, prospect park, vinegar hill

Hop off the Brooklyn Bridge pedestrian pathway and you'll find a queue into Brooklyn's established culinary scene. West of the Brooklyn Navy Yard and east of Dumbo (Down Under the Manhattan Bridge Overpass), Vinegar Hill is a quaint neighborhood with Greek Revival-style row houses. In Fort Greene and Prospect Heights, tree-lined streets and sports utility baby strollers elicit a slower pace compared to its northern hipster precincts. Daily joggers have Prospect Park and Brooklyn Botanical Garden, while other healthy types make beelines to the many yoga studios nearby. Within the 478-plus manicured acres of Park Slope's Green-Wood Cemetery – a national historic landmark – you'll find the highest city viewpoint in Brooklyn. Clinton Hill, with its lavish old Beaux-Arts style houses, is home to film stars and musicians as well as Barclays Center and Brooklyn Academy of Music, the oldest performing multi-arts center in the country.

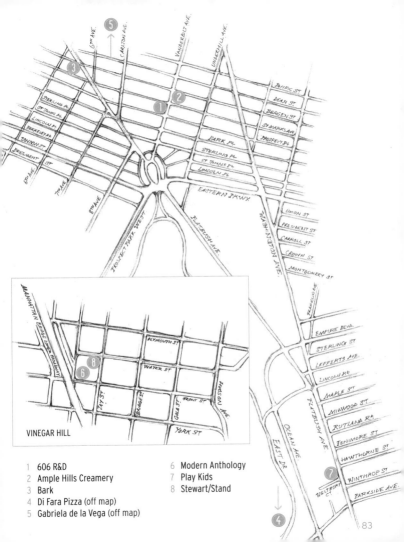

1 606 R&D
2 Ample Hills Creamery
3 Bark
4 Di Fara Pizza (off map)
5 Gabriela de la Vega (off map)

6 Modern Anthology
7 Play Kids
8 Stewart/Stand

VINEGAR HILL

83

606 R&D

Simple American food with a twist

606 Vanderbilt Avenue (between St Marks and Prospect)
+1 718 230 0125 / 606vanderbiltbklyn.com / Open daily

The morning after a booze-soaked work party (on a Tuesday night, no less), a co-worker brought in a huge box of the most ethereal cake donuts from 606 R&D. A dyed-in-the-wool donut devotee, I was converted. When I finally got the chance to make the trek to Prospect Heights for their weekly, family-style Sunday Supper, I became a true believer. I also learned my new church has a lot more to offer than just coffee and amazing donuts. There's no better way to close out a weekend than a simple meal of roast chicken, mac and cheese, and a big green salad here, shared with a few friends, perhaps in the adorable patio space, where you could be at a backyard barbecue. This is the kind of neighborhood spot that's worth going out of your way to find.

AMPLE HILLS CREAMERY

Organic ice cream and classic sundae shop goodness

623 Vanderbilt Avenue (between St Marks and Prospect)
+1 347 240 3926 / amplehills.com / Open daily

The weekend that Ample Hills opened, I walked by on a sweltering night around 7pm and saw a line around the corner. Thinking that the crowd was just there to cool off, I had a giggle at the name and kept moving, telling myself that a popsicle would work just as well. When I finally got to try a scoop of Ample's chocolate ice cream and another of salted caramel, I knew I had misinterpreted the reason for that line. Super fresh organic cream and bold, salt-forward swirls of flavor put this frozen goodness head and shoulders above anything you'll find in the supermarket, or in many other ice cream shops, for that matter.

BARK

Classic NY hot dogs

474 Bergen Street (between 5th and 6th) / **+1 718 789 1939**
barkhotdogs.com / **Open daily**

Some of the many travelers to New York arrive with a hard-core determination to discover everything on their personalized hit list. It may be visiting the Empire State building; walking through Central Park; or of course, eating the quintessential corner stand hot dog. But it should be pointed out that not all dogs are created equal. In fact, Bark's hot dogs are locally sourced from Hartmann's Old World Sausage Company in upstate NY. The links are juicy, flavorful and come with 12 different types of relishes, mustards, sauces and toppings, and a snappy bite. And for those who will ever favor burgers over hot dogs, Bark cooks up a humdinger of a patty, made with all-Angus beef.

DI FARA PIZZA

Iconic Neapolitan-style pizza

1424 Avenue J (at East 15th) / +1 718 258 1367 / difara.com
Open daily

Every NY pizzeria has their own modus operandi, whether it's Tottono's with their grandfathered coal oven, Franny's for their chewy crust, or Lombardi's for its history. That said, no other cult following compares to the magic at Di Fara's. Die-hard pie fans endure incredible queues, as they watch 77-year-old Dom DeMarco hand toss and assemble every pizza by hand, feeding the flames within his 1,000-degree oven. Fans salivate as they watch his flour-coated scissors snip at basil leaves with Pollack-like caprice. Dom uses genuine Neapolitan-style ingredients: buffalo mozzarella, 00-flour and San Marzano tomatoes, and when it comes to his square pizzas many vow it's "worth the wait." Indeed, whether waiting for a table or anticipating a return visit, Di Fara's motto will always ring true.

GABRIELA DE LA VEGA

Handcrafted jewelry and chic garments

88 South Portland Avenue (between Lafayette and Fulton)
+1 718 858 1152 / gabrieladelavega.bigcartel.com / Closed Monday

Gabriela de la Vega is not a believer in trends. Who she is and what she represents is based on quintessential and timeless beauty. A pioneering self-taught designer, her intuitions blasted her into jewelry stardom in the 1990's, when she began wholesaling for Barneys and all over the world. Nearly a decade later Gabriela opened a boutique, carrying her own range of aesthetically irresistible organic jewelry as well as a range of inspiring clothes from A Détacher and her mother's cement botanical sculptures. Gabriela's aesthetic is effortlessly organic and delicately precise. Juxtaposing her jewelry with vintage, dainty, delicate and robust materials makes it difficult for even the most reticent buyer to resist leaving without a single purchase.

MODERN ANTHOLOGY

Men's compendium of design

68 Jay Street (between Water and Front) / +1 718 558 3020
modernanthology.com / Open daily

Modern Anthology has an extraordinary collection of retro treasures of form
and function. A meander through the store is like simultaneously walking
through the Smithsonian and the Museum of Natural History both at once,
thanks to an array of topography maps, old-fashioned outdoor apparatuses
and furry friends in taxidermy heaven. A flashback of childhood is found in
many knickknacks, whether it's vintage dice or filament bulbs. This boutique
has an emphasis on timeless, masculine and handsome designs, and also
carries gifts of adult whimsy: Max Poglia handmade knives, leather goods
and mid-century modern furniture.

PLAY KIDS

Smart toys for smart kids

676 Flatbush Avenue (between Westbury and Hawthorne)
+1 347 715 9347 / playkidsstore.com / Open daily

There once was a time when playthings were made of solid, indestructible materials. A time when kids played rough, yet at the end of the day no tears were shed over a broken wing or a missing glass eye. At Play Kids, it's the parents who step inside first, with youngsters in tow. This is no ordinary toy store. Owners Shelley Kramer and Carl Blake make it a point to carry playthings that last. They also want children to get optimal enjoyment from their products, so they offer daily workshops and events. From drum-alongs to sing-alongs, this is a place for those looking for something rather more than just temporal toys.

STEWART/STAND

Modern accessories

141A Front Street (between Pearl and Jay) / +1 718 875 1204
stewartstanddesignstore.com / Open daily

After brothers Theo and Paul Stewart-Stand successfully launched the ingenious wallet that prevented identity fraud, Theo's wife, Penelope Mahot, took over, turning the once gadget-focused gift shop into a playful and endearing boutique. Penelope recalls how Stewart/Stand's own label developed and flourished, and now wants to showcase up-and-coming designers herself. That's why roughly a third of the products found here are locally designed, such as Mia and Finn's sought after hand-block prints. She breathes life and respect into her environment, as she consciously curates PVC- and animal-cruelty-free pieces.

public markets

Locavore havens

BROOKLYN FLEA MARKET & SMORGASBURG
80 North 5th Street (at Wythe), weekends (winter)
90 Kent Avenue (at North 7th), Saturday (summer) and
Brooklyn Bridge Park's Pier 5, Sunday (summer), brooklynflea.com

ESSEX STREET MARKET
120 Essex Street, +1 212 312 3603, essexstreetmarket.com, open daily

FORT GREENE FLEA MARKET
176 Lafayette Street (between Clermont and Vanderbilt)
brooklynflea.com, Saturday (summer)

NEW AMSTERDAM MARKET
South Street (between Beekman and Peck Slip), +1 212 766 8688
newamsterdammarket.org, Sunday

THE CHELSEA MARKET
75 9th Street (between 15th and 16th), chelseamarket.com, open daily

Outdoor markets, such as the summer **Brooklyn Flea Market & Smorgasburg** and **Fort Greene Flea Market**, are wildly popular with folks seeking out priceless antiques from amongst kitsch bric-a-brac, or foodies hunting the best local fare. There's also a strong sense of community between the vendors.

New Amsterdam Market (in the previous home of the historic Fulton Fish Market) showcases local farm produce and artisanal goods. With stands changing every Sunday, one can find all sorts of treats, from flaky chicken pot pies to handmade cutting boards.

I prefer eating al fresco on sunny days, but in winter I escape indoors at **Brooklyn Flea Market & Smorgasburg**, in a huge 50,000-square-foot space where over 100 vendors cozy up next to 50 brick-and-mortar businesses. Worldly renowned for its impressive food hall, **Chelsea Market** offers cuisines ranging from Bánh Mì sandwiches to fresh masa tortillas, and Thai curries to ice cream from local dairy farms.

For something more traditional, the **Essex Street Market**, originally housing push-carts in the 1940s, now hosts respected vendors who've sold their prime cuts, fresh fish, cheeses, breads and tropical fruits for several generations.

NEW AMSTERDAM MARKET

williamsburg and greenpoint

bushwick, bedford-stuyvesant

Thousands of Lower East Side residents crossed the Williamsburg Bridge in 1903, relocating to Bedford-Stuyvesant and South and East Williamsburg. Today, folks may grimace when taking the so-called "G-eriatric" G-train, which runs the longitude of Brooklyn rather than directly into Manhattan. Yet, it seems Millennials have no qualms in humble-bragging about their epic commute. Once dubbed the "Third hippest neighborhood in the country" by *Forbes* magazine, the area continues to test trends and embodies a youthful energy. Despite hipster affectations, it's worth visiting Little Poland in Greenpoint for warm pierogi or donuts on Manhattan Avenue. Williamsburg also has some great spots for admiring the skyline of Manhattan, namely the view from the East River Ferry (pg 128) or from Wythe Hotel's rooftop bar, The Ides (pg 8).

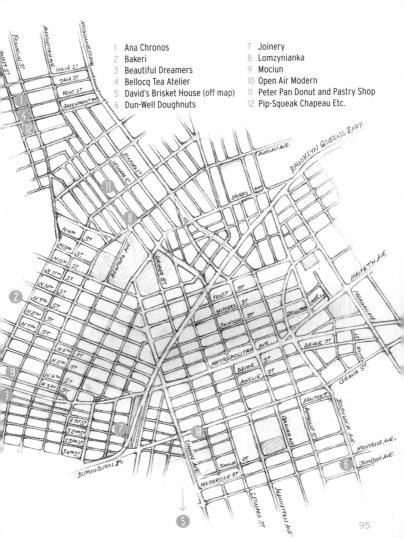

1 Ana Chronos
2 Bakeri
3 Beautiful Dreamers
4 Bellocq Tea Atelier
5 David's Brisket House (off map)
6 Dun-Well Doughnuts
7 Joinery
8 Lomzynianka
9 Mociun
10 Open Air Modern
11 Peter Pan Donut and Pastry Shop
12 Pip-Squeak Chapeau Etc.

ANA CHRONOS

Mint condition vintage gowns

135 Franklin Street (between Kent and Greenpoint)
+1 718 433 1020   anachronosnyc.com
Open Wednesday–Sunday; Monday and Tuesday by appointment

My mother nicknamed me "mole", because I'd rummage through her armoire trying on, and eventually "permanently borrowing", her designer pieces. At Ana Chronos, owner Erica Dobbs may not have been as culpable as yours truly, but her eagle eye has helped create a beautiful, era-structured shop that's reminiscent of an elegant, walk-in closet. Inspired by her fashion-forward grandmother, Dobbs' offerings range from a 1920's hand-painted, silk kimono to a slew of 1980's Christian Lacroix. It's nice to finally walk into a vintage store that's articulate, graceful and as sternly organized as my mother's closet — well, up until I walk in.

BAKERI

Lovingly made goods

150 Wythe Avenue (between 7th and 8th) / **+1 718 388 8037**
bakeribrooklyn.com / **Open daily**

In my dream life, in which I'm a neurosurgeon with loads of free time,
I get up at 4am to make gorgeous loaves of hand-shaped bread, platters
of frittata and baskets of muffins. I'd do all this myself because, when it
comes down to it, homemade is just better. Or so I thought until I went
to Bakeri, where my dream life and real life collided spectacularly. This
collective of cool girls make dreamy baked goods that rival grandma's.
Enjoy them in the cozy dining area, have some outside in their garden, or
take them home and pretend you made them yourself. A word to the wise:
no need to wake up pre-sunrise, but they do have a tendency to sell out, so
get there early for the best selection.

BEAUTIFUL DREAMERS

A new home for the bobo-chic

326 Wythe Avenue (between South 1st and Grand) / **+1 917 687 7959**
beautifuldreamers.com / **Open daily**

Beautiful Dreamers is a whirlwind of striking mysticism and bobo-chic that gathers its silky frayed seams with a sense of great profundity. Co-owners April Hughes and Marina Burini offer a hypnotic kaleidoscope of colors and textures that whispers influences of the likes of Paul Poiret. Handmade birch racks intertwined with leather make you feel as if you've stepped inside the abode of an alpinist with exquisitely sharp taste. Beautiful Dreamers feels like a far-off land where textile alchemy could exist.

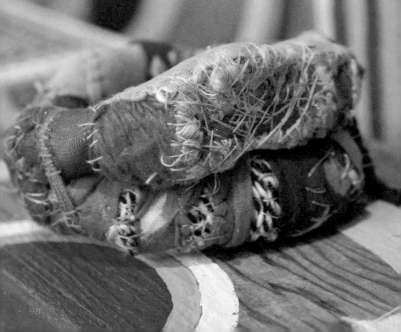

BELLOCQ TEA ATELIER

Leaves parfumerie

104 West Street (corner of Kent) / +1 800 495 5416 / bellocq.com
Closed Tuesday

From the rich yolk-colored packaging, to the evocative names, to the smell and taste of the blends, Bellocq tea is transporting. Inhale the White Wolf and you're wandering a winter-bright forest in Russia, all pine and snow. The Queen's Guard is floral, but the rose and lavender soften the strong backbone of the black Ceylon. What I'm addicted to, though, is the Earl Grey as I've never had it before: fresh Sicilian bergamot oil puts imitators to shame, and it just needs a touch of cream to be an ease to any worry.

DAVID'S BRISKET HOUSE

Bona fide pastrami sandwiches

533 Nostrand Avenue (between Herkimer and Atlantic)
+1 718 789 1155 / davidsbriskethouseinc.com / **Open daily**

Though I live on the same street as beloved Katz's Delicatessen, seeing
that endless line encourages me to venture elsewhere for my briny
pastrami and corned beef. Who knew a staunch standby would be in
Bedstuy (Bedford-Stuyvesant, for long). David's brisket sandwich is
layered a mile high, with a side of luxurious jus, for half the price. If that
doesn't pacify a hungry stomach or loud mouth, I don't know what will.
In a neighborhood primarily populated with West African and fried
chicken cuisine, there's still a lunch line. The only difference is, rather
than camera frenzied tourists, you'll wait alongside locals, some of
whom have been coming here since the 1960's.

DUN-WELL DOUGHNUTS

Vegan donuts done well

222 Montrose Avenue (between Humboldt and Bushwick)
+1 347 294 0871 / dunwelldoughnuts.com / Open daily

Vegan isn't really in my vocabulary, but when donuts are this pillowy, with crisp exteriors and a plush crumb, who cares what's not in them? Dun-Well is all soda-shop charm meets lumberjack hipster: expect food to be served on a round of wood, by a man wearing a bowtie and striped shirt. Those exemplary donuts are the main draw, but the creative duo behind this operation also whips up ice cream, soda syrups and savory snacks. And since there are no animal products to be found, feel free to convince yourself it's healthy, too.

JOINERY

Global designer treasures

263 South 1st Street (between Havemeyer and Marcy)
+1 347 889 6164 / joinerynyc.com / **Open daily**

Growing up in a small town, I became an exclusive catalog kid. I
went behind my parents' back, splurging months' worth of hoarded
lunch funds to purchase pieces available exclusively in major cities.
Flipping through Joinery's hangers reminded me of learning about
global fashion trends from catalogs past. The shop welcomes a bevy of
international designers, such as London's Folk, ffiXXed from Shenzhen
and Parisian Hixsept. Owner Angela Silva's cultural embrace is also
displayed in her hand-torched, pine ceiling (shou sugi ban, a Japanese
technique). Just as cataloging once did, Joinery allows me to live
vicariously in the world of fashion.

LOMZYNIANKA

Authentic homestyle Polish cuisine

646 Manhattan Avenue (between Nassau and Norman)
+1 718 389 9439 / lomzynianka.com / Open daily

In Greenpoint, because everyone speaks enthusiastically in Polish, it feels like Warsaw is just around the corner. I played the tourist card one day and asked two Polish apoteke owners, resting out front in their fold-out chairs, where to find homemade pierogi. They spouted some names, and then began a cacophonous debate on whose recommendation was best. Endorsement No. 1 happened to be Lomzynianka. Named after Poland's northeastern city, Lomza, this family owned restaurant is known for juicy kielbasas (sausages), creamy pierogi and crispy potato pancakes. The food is pleasingly simple, and a good bowl of borscht, bright, sharp and sweet, is something I'd defend in a loud verbal dispute any day.

mociun

Scandinavian-inspired boutique

224 Wythe Avenue (corner of North 4th) / **+1 718 387 3731**
mociun.com / **Open daily**

This storefront may be mistaken for a pristine art gallery, but look closer and you'll find Doug Johnston's chorded merchandise playfully displayed across the store's glossy cement floor, atop windowsills, underneath tables and against stark white walls. Getting down on one's knees to test out floor pillows by Shabd or the shape of Eric Bonnin's ceramics feels like visiting the minimalist abode of that stylish friend you secretly envy. That "stylish friend" is designer and storeowner Caitlin Mociun, who just so happens to seek one-of-a-kind pieces created by small, local designers; some whose studios are their kitchen tables. Mociun is a place of constant rumination, inspiration and progression.

OPEN AIR MODERN

Danish 20th-century furniture and rare books

489 Lorimer Street (between Grand and Powers) / +1 718 383 6465
openairmodern.com / Closed Monday

My love for Scandinavian design comes from my father, an architect whose trundle beds and dining nooks look like something from a Carl Larsson painting. From there, it was just a hop and a skip and an art major to a full-blown obsession with all things mid-20th-century and Danish. Open Air Modern owner Matt Singer, shares my obsession and stocks his airy rehabbed garage with mint condition pieces. I'd love to fill my apartment with his lust-worthy furniture, all burnished wood tones and modern silhouettes, but while I try to save up, it's the vintage Dansk tableware and the hard-to-find art and design books that keep me coming back for more.

PETER PAN DONUT AND PASTRY SHOP

Old-school bakery

727 Manhattan Avenue (between Norman and Meserole)
+1 718 389 3676 / peterpan-donuts.com / Open daily

Three words on why I find myself commuting over to Brooklyn on that fickle G train: Bavarian Cream donuts. For just a dollar, you'll get five of these yummy rings – take that McMunchies menu. This bakery, over 60 years old, is home to old grandpas parked on stools, ordering their usual in a stream of Polish, while the to-go line, snaking out the door, consists of 20-something hipsters 'tagging' and 'checking-in'. It seems that Peter Pan Donut and Pastry Shop never grew out of old New York. The irresistible charm of original décor and mid-century pricing can't help but make you feel as though you've just visited Neverland.

PIP-SQUEAK CHAPEAU ETC.

Linen sophisticates

99 Franklin Street (between Milton and Noble) / +1 917 270 5184
pip-squeakchapeau.com / Closed Monday and Tuesday

At Pip-Squeak Chapeau Etc., you'll seek comfort in the crinkling of natural fibers found in designer Sveta Kazakova's pieces. She emphasizes that clothing should be more about how one feels, rather than devoting time to fashion norms. With summer heat hitting triple digits, I wish I shared the moxie of NYC women on GoTopless Day, but I'll stick to Sveta's A-line tanks of billowing, cool linen that won't adhere to sweaty skin. Her no-frill designs exude elegance, like crow's feet formed from a gentle smile. It's the subtleties that speak for generations, and her pieces of simplicity and grace will surely last a lifetime.

JOSEPH BEUYS, 7000 OAKS
West 22nd Street (between 10th and 11th), +1 212 989 5566
diaart.org

NOGUCHI MUSEUM
9-01 33rd Road (between Vernon and 10th), +1 718 204 7088
noguchi.org, closed Monday and Tuesday

THE CLOISTERS
99 Margaret Corbin Drive (Fort Tryon Park), +1 212 923 3700
metmuseum.org/visit/visit-the-cloisters, open daily

THE MORGAN LIBRARY AND MUSEUM
225 Madison Avenue (at 36th Street), +1 212 685 0008
themorgan.org, closed Monday

WALTER DE MARIA, THE NEW YORK EARTH ROOM
141 Wooster Street (between Prince and Houston), +1 212 989 5566
diaart.org, open Wednesday-Sunday, September-June

WALTER DE MARIA, THE BROKEN KILOMETER
393 West Broadway (between Spring and Broome), +1 212 989 5566
diaart.org, open Wednesday-Sunday, September-June

museums and galleries

Niche miscellanies and installation art

History whispers to you from every hallway of
The Morgan Library and Museum. As well as priceless artworks,
J.P. Morgan's personal collection of rarities and originals includes artifacts
such as Mozart's original, hand-quilled scores; Hemingway's ornery
correspondence and the Sforza family taro cards from 1490.

Past Tryon State Park and overlooking the Hudson River **The Cloisters**, a
branch of The Metropolitan Museum, holds over 5,000 medieval European
works, including the famed Unicorn Tapestries. Stained glass and gold
triptychs extend throughout the rooms, underpinning the ecclesiastical aura
that resonates within the medieval monastery's five transcendent cloisters.

In Queens, the eponymous **Noguchi Museum** in Long Island City, was
designed and created by the Japanese-American sculptor to display his own
works. The adjoining sculpture garden is a magical place that resets buzzing
creative minds with its calming, basalt stone carvings.

Although SoHo may now resemble a gigantic shopping mall, glimpses of its
artistic, bohemian past remain. On the second floor of a 3,600-square-foot
loft is **Walter De Maria's** *The New York Earth Room*, a sculpture consisting
of 280,000 pounds of lush soil, lying 22-inches deep. Within walking distance
is another De Maria installation, ***The Broken Kilometer***: a room filled with
500 polished, solid brass rods that, if assembled, would measure exactly
3,280 feet long. Moving over to Chelsea, **Joseph Beuys'** *7000 Oaks*, is
a continuing art project where multiple species of trees accompanied
with basalt stone columns are planted to signify urban renewal and
environmental social change.

long island city and astoria

woodside, sunnyside

Though there are five train lines that make stops
in Long Island City, this neighborhood is often
overlooked as a go-to destination. As home to
Silvercup Studios, which cleverly sensationalizes
NYC pop culture into every program it produces
(*Sex in the City*, *30 Rock*, to name but two);
The American Museum of the Moving Image;
experimental exhibition space MoMA PS1; and
art house The SPACE L.I.C., it is an epicenter for
filmmakers and artists alike. There are also plenty
of hidden-gem ethnic eateries that'll tempt visitors
to dinner before seducing them into signing a
year's lease in the neighborhood after dessert.

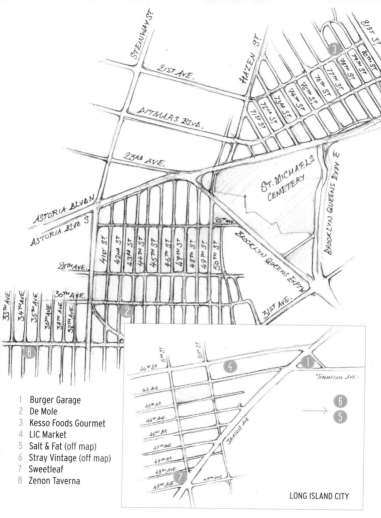

1 Burger Garage
2 De Mole
3 Kesso Foods Gourmet
4 LIC Market
5 Salt & Fat (off map)
6 Stray Vintage (off map)
7 Sweetleaf
8 Zenon Taverna

LONG ISLAND CITY

BURGER GARAGE

Quality sandwich pit stop

25-36 Jackson Avenue (corner of 44th) / +1 718 392 0424
theburgergarage.com / Closed Sunday

This is a burger joint for both the purist and the friend who always asks if the
kitchen can "caramelize the onions". It's a place where the accommodating
service staff has no qualms in adding to the long list of accouterments off
the seasonal board, or adapting to dietary requirements including gluten
intolerance. Using fresh, ground meats from local celebrity butcher Pat
LaFrieda, Burger Garage doesn't skimp when forming a quarter-pound of
pure Angus Beef brisket, chuck and prime rib cuts. Caloric intake increases
as one gets into savory sautéed mushrooms and fried egg topping territory.
And you needn't miss out on Sundays: you can find Burger Garage at the
Long Island City Flea & Food Market on 46th Avenue (at 5th).

DE MOLE

Pueblan cuisine from the home country

42–20 30th Avenue (corner of 43rd) / **+1 718 777 1655**
demolenyc.com / **Open daily**

I recall taking frequent family trips to Seoul as a kid, when my mother would check in multiple empty suitcases, zipped one within another like Russian dolls, for the sole purpose of hoarding back kombu, anchovies and squid. "It tastes better from the Korean seashore," she'd say. Like her, part owner and chef Ramiro Mendez flies back ingredients from his homeland, Santa Inés Ahuatempan, Puebla, including the impressive 17 that he uses in his robust signature mole. Truth be told, you can't go wrong when fresh ingredients are paired with passed-down family recipes. Sure, there's a time and place for the corner taqueria stand, but it can't compete when a craving for sweet and spicy mole and zippy hibiscus fresca strikes.

KESSO FOODS GOURMET

Finest homemade Greek yogurt

7720 21st Avenue (between 77th and 78th) / +1 718 777 5303
No website / Closed Saturday and Sunday

I believe the search for something good is worth any journey, even if it means a bus transfer from a train station. Yes — I said bus and train in the same sentence. Let's just say it's not as arduous as Odysseus traveling across the Anatolia. Stavro Kessissogloo runs this tiny, unassuming store and makes 400 gallons of Greek yogurt daily. The majority is distributed to neighboring Greek restaurants, but the rest of his super fresh, silky yogurt he sells by the quart or spoonful, topped with granola, honey and fresh fruit. In addition, homemade kataifi, kanafeh and other sweet and flaky pastries are alluringly lined up in the glass case. Such indulgence makes it well worth the journey, and the blissful return home.

LIC MARKET

Locavore hot spot

21-52 44th Drive (west of 23rd Street) / +1 718 361 0013
licmarket.com / Open daily

LIC Market is not your typical 200-seat, cacophonous, 100 dollars-a-head NYC restaurant. In fact, it feels like a gourmand's home. Its foyer is converted into a diner, and the fragrant scent of herbs tickles the senses on the walk down the hall to the eight tables in the back room. Owner and chef Alex Schindler prepares specials everyday for loyal regulars and commuters alike. Preparing everything fresh within a 24-hour period; carrying strictly seasonal produce; and using only hormone- and antibiotic-free provisions, this is a place that makes one consider becoming an official local regular.

SALT & FAT

Modern Asian-American cuisine

41-16 Queens Boulevard (between 41st and 42nd)
+1 718 433 3702 / saltandfatny.com / **Closed Monday**

Chocolate and peanut butter, Champagne and oysters, Chanel and Karl Lagerfield are life's most ingenious combinations. But salt and fat is the intrinsic, ambrosial apogee of what is so mouthwatering about anything fried, cured and rendered. Chef Daniel Yi conjures irresistible, knee-buckling amalgams such as the amuse-bouche of popcorn popped in duck fat, which immediately makes you wonder what other hedonistic turns dinner may take. The paper-thin, caramelized hard sear of succulent diver scallops and the candy-like crunchy fried chicken paired with *kakdugi* (pickled Korean radish), are but some exquisite examples of how Salt & Fat balances the delicate techniques of modern American cuisine with an underlying piquant streak of Asian flavors.

STRAY VINTAGE

Treasures far from abandonment

4809 Skillman Avenue (between 48th and 49th) / **+1 718 779 7795**
strayvintage.wordpress.com / **Closed Monday**

This mid-century vintage store, housing second hand homewares neatly
laid out in organized fashion, feels like a hip grandmother's cottage.
There's everything from cherry-wood chairs, to various beveled mirrors
hanging along the wall, and even an assortment of reasonably priced
pre-prohibition stemware. You can imagine hip grandma passing you a
Manhattan in a mint-condition, etched cocktail glass. Stray Vintage is
different from other second hand stores, because there is no need for
treasure "hunting" here. It's all perfectly laid out, and pieces happen to
spontaneously land in one's eager grasp, each one so pristinely pretty
that you just know its next home will most likely be its last.

SWEETLEAF

The church of coffee

10-93 Jackson Avenue (corner of 11th) / **+1 917 832 6726**
sweetleaflic.com / **Open daily**

Every time I visit any one of Long Island City's day-trip destinations, such as MoMA P.S. 1, I always end up at Sweetleaf. I used to think it was the comforting ambiance of the space, or the perfectly extracted espresso from "Dorothy", the La Marzocco Linea machine, but I've discovered it's really the carrot cake that keeps me coming back drooling. Pastry authority Beverly Lauchner bakes everything in house, from the fluffy, cinnamon and granulated sugar coated donuts to that life-changing carrot cake. Coffee connoisseurs rejoice, as owner Freddy stocks bags from the Northwest, from Heart Coffee to Stumptown beans.

ZENON TAVERNA

Family-owned Cypriot cuisine

3410 31st Avenue (between 34th and 35th) / +1 718 956 0133
zenontaverna.com / Open daily

On this street of Astoria let the wafts of grilled seafood, citrus and rose water guide you to Zenon Taverna. Co-owners Dora and Stelios Papageorgiou dish up Cypriot cuisine, and after 24 years, Stelios can still be found greeting customers with a warm smile, sharing joyful tapestry-like stories, as if they are guests at his daughter's wedding. While Dora runs the kitchen, the buoyant Stelios can be found making his daily 5am outings to the local fish market, where vendors always set aside the freshest fish for "Junior". The crispy, succulent, char-grilled octopus is worth adding on to the 16 gorgeous dishes that already make up the notable Kypriaki Mezedes platter, including *tarama* (red caviar) and *ortikia* (quail eggs). The bottom of the menu reads "Siga-siga", meaning "Slowly-slowly". No rushing the smorgasbord here.

jackson heights and corona

elmhurst, murray hill, forest hills

Queens is a wonderful mish-mash of immigrant
Southeast Asian, Latino and Indian cultures and
cuisines. The infamous 7 Train runs parallel through
Roosevelt Boulevard, the main artery where you'll
find fresh Thai food, multiple ceviche stands and
a lady who flips arepas until 5am. The 7 Train's
penultimate stop is in Flushing: handy for tennis
buffs in town for the U.S. Open and where Chinese
dumplings reign. The residential hum of lawnmowers
and exotic aromas from crispy panipuri emanate
throughout Jackson Heights. Koreatown on
Northern Boulevard and 149th Place, in Murray Hill,
is filled with karaoke bars, barbecue restaurants,
refreshing naengmyeon and dirt cheap soju. The
densely populated storefront signs (sans English),
along with the aroma of spices, are telltale signs of
authentic culinary fare — and it's all just a 30-minute
commute from Grand Central Station.

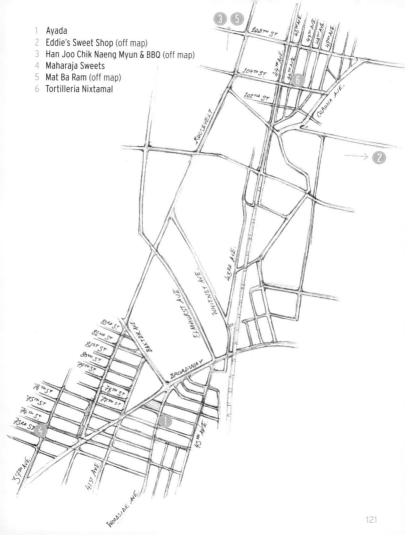

AYADA

Homestyle Thai

77-08 Woodside Avenue (between 77th and 78th)   +1 718 424 0844
No website / Open daily

An old schoolmate of mine, who'd left her family in Thailand to open a restaurant, once explained how to rate a Thai restaurant based on its spicy star indicator system. Through her tutelage I'd find myself inherently skeptical when four stars denied a sweat mustache, and no star became a just cause to break open a bottle of Pepto. Ayada sits quietly on a residential street, and Chef Duangjai Thammasat specializes in northeastern Thai cuisine. Using only fresh chilies, Ayada's two stars will make you want to order a glass of beer – or two – so you can grin and very happily bear the delicious spiciness.

EDDIE'S SWEET SHOP

Turn of the century ice cream parlor

105-29 Metropolitan Avenue (corner of 72nd) / +1 718 520 8514
No website / Closed Monday

I almost had a major meltdown when I tasted Eddie's Sweet Shop's ice cream. Over dramatic? Not even close. Just one sip from a cream soda induced a flashback to tasting malted chocolate for the very first time. Vito Citrano has run the shop since the late 1960s, improving past recipes and making everything from flavored syrups to butterscotch sauce by hand. Having had only four owners since the turn of the 20th century, Eddie's Sweet Shop's original hardware remains untouched, from the leather bound stools to the 1920s icebox freezers. Whether it's an orange cream or a banana split, such vivid euphoria of saccharine bliss just might trigger creamery catharsis.

HAN JOO CHIK NAENG MYUN & BBQ

Samgyeopsal barbecue specialist

41-06 149th Place (between 41st and Barclay) / +1 718 359 6888
No website / Open daily

For 360 days of the year, my fastidious mother cooked strictly Korean meals. The remaining few meals were eaten out, at Korean restaurants. Leaving my mother's venerable prep table to rest allowed me a chance to order delectable obscurities: "Let's order something mom wouldn't make…" sounds less insulting in Korean. The trade-off often involved listening to my mother's critique of how dinner was heavily salted. Once choosing my meals more independently, it wasn't until a visit to Han Joo Chik Naeng Myun & BBQ, while eating crispy pork belly, when I recalled the same discerning tastes and standards from childhood. The seasonal specialties, such as naengmyeon with springtime turnip-greens kimchi, or the standard classics will surely not disappoint the adventurous eater, nor the industrious Korean mother.

MAHARAJA SWEETS

Homemade Indian treats and desserts

7310 37th Avenue (between 73rd and 74th) / +1 718 505 2680
maharajasweet.com / Open daily

Aside from their delicious chaat, Maharaja Sweets is best known for the comprehensive assortment of authentic Punjabi and Bangladeshi desserts sold by the pound. The restaurant and shop is tucked away within the sweet spot of Jackson Heights (or Little India). Barfi studded with pistachios or perfumed with rose water melts at the touch of the tongue. The ras malai is fresh, creamy and has developed a cult following. There's usually a line out the door for their beautiful gift boxes filled with colorful sugary treats, but trust me, these morsels prove good things do come to those who wait.

MAT BA RAM

Knife cut Korean noodle shop

150-40 Northern Boulevard (between 150th and Murray)
+1 718 460 2535 / No website / Open daily

One balmy summer evening in Seoul, my aunt asked if I enjoyed kalguksoo. It's too hot for soup, I thought. Auntie grinned, instructed me to secure my seatbelt, and zipped along the highway straight to the coast. She insisted the sea air and briny broth went hand in hand, and that finding a "kalguksoo master" warranted the hour-long drive for noodles at 11pm on a Tuesday. A similar 45-minute commute from Penn Station to Mat Ba Ram is rewarded by chef and owner Amy Jung's springy noodles, refreshing broth and fluffy, hand-torn dumplings, all reminiscent of the Incheon Coast.

TORTILLERIA NIXTAMAL

Masa tortillas made from scratch

104-05 47th Avenue (between 104th and 108th) / **+1 718 699 2434**
tortillerianixtamal.com / **Open daily**

Stepping into Tortilleria Nixtamal's underground prep kitchen, it's hard to believe that such a tiny space stores, soaks, cooks and grinds whole kernels of hominy, and churns out 1,600 pounds of creamy masa every day. Owner Shauna Page says the tortilla machine, manufactured in and flown over from Mexico, produces 30,000 organic, kosher disks daily, which are delivered to more than 50 local businesses. For the restaurant, only local meat, seafood, cheese and naturally rendered lard are used and while NY lunches are notoriously hasty, here the pace is as indulgent as their creamy tamales. So I certainly have no qualms in ordering another round of tacos, as I wait for my tortillas to be weighed and packed up.

tranquil spaces

Pockets of solace for stressed souls

For respite from the cacophonous symphony that is NY's cultural soundtrack, start with a walk above the city on **The High Line** (pg 80), and then take the A-Train to **Fort Tryon Park**, where you'll be surrounded by ferns and alpine plants.

Gloriously peaceful afternoons are also on hand via a free ferry ride to **Governors Island**. There, 172 acres of bicycle paths; blankets of plush grass; natural turf ball-fields; and 50 hammocks await you. Plus there's the FIGMENT interactive sculpture garden, an imaginative art display.

For just four dollars, hop on the **East River Ferry** (ERF), especially when summer's viscous humidity incubates the Metro. Literally a breath of fresh air, the ERF departs from Wall Street to East 34th Street; its route between Brooklyn and Queens offering magnificent skyline views, and only the meditative rippling sounds of water along with the gentle hum of the engine can be heard.

Those wishing for some quiet reflection and to pay homage to iconic New Yorkers such as Jean-Michel Basquiat and Leonard Bernstein, should head to the 478-acre **Green-Wood Cemetery**. Lauded as having the highest viewpoint in Brooklyn, Green-Wood's manicured landscape is perfect for peaceful, contemplative strolls.

EAST RIVER FERRY
From Wall Street to East 34th Street, eastriverferry.com, daily

FORT TRYON PARK
West 192nd Street to Dyckman Street, forttryonparktrust.org
open daily

GOVERNORS ISLAND
Ferry from Battery Maritime Building, 10 South Street
govisland.com, open daily, May–September

GREEN-WOOD CEMETERY
500 25th Street (at 5th Avenue), green-wood.com, open daily